Presented to

_____

By

_____

Date

_____

THE
TRUTH
DIARY

Dennis J. Carothers
Andrew B. Miller

seedbed

SOWING FOR A GREAT AWAKENING

Printed in the United States of America

Paperback ISBN: 978-1-62824-075-7
Mobi ISBN: 978-1-62824-076-4
ePub ISBN: 978-1-62824-077-1
uPDF ISBN: 978-1-62824-078-8

Library of Congress Control Number: 2014947570

Cover calligraphy by Laurie Soileau Schlisner
Cover design by Brushfire Design Studio

Note to the reader: The author has capitalized the deity pronouns in the Scripture quotations throughout the text to match the style of the narrative.

SEEDBED PUBLISHING
Franklin, Tennessee
Seedbed.com
SOWING FOR A GREAT AWAKENING

THE HISTORY OF GOD AND THE HUMAN RACE

For God so loved the world that he gave his one and only Son, that whoever believes in him shall not perish but have eternal life.

John 3:16

Prologue

IN THE BEGINNING

Millenniums ago and prior to the inception of life on earth, the Creator God, maker and designer of the heavens and the earth, chose to create the very first human.

God created a living being made of flesh and blood that He could love and be loved by. The ability to receive love and to give love was the paramount characteristic of this first human. This wonderful and amazing being was called "man."

God walked on the earth side by side with His magnificent new creation.

A beautiful friendship was developing between God and man as they walked together in the garden paradise that God had created especially for him.

Sadly a day came when, in a tragic act of disobedience, this, the first man rejected God's authority and became lost on the earth.

Dear reader, please know this, you and I are descendants of this rebellious man. If you have ever made mistakes, felt lost, lonely, empty, or like something is missing in your life, you will understand this story.

God's close and loving relationship with man is told in a few short pages at the beginning of the book of Genesis. The entire remainder of the Bible chronicles God's attempt as a loving Father to reconcile man back to Himself; God's journey with man culminates in the arrival on earth of a glorious Redeemer who would make a way for man to be reunited back to God.

This is God's account of how human life began as found in the ancient, divinely inspired words of the Bible. The following pages contain a condensed paraphrase of God's history with His human creation. The presentation is God speaking in the first person.

I

The Invitation

I formed man from the dirt of the earth. I breathed life into his newly formed lungs and called him *Adam*, which means "red clay man" (Gen. 2:7).

I alone was Adam's Father and Maker.

I loved Adam as My son and Adam loved Me as his Father. I created Adam with a conscience and the ability to choose. My love was unconditional. Adam could choose to love Me, or not.

A beautiful garden paradise was made for him with trees and flowers of every kind. The trees of the garden bore perfect and delicious fruit. This garden I called Eden was serene and beautiful.

Coming down from heaven, I would spend time walking with Adam in the cool of the evening. Together we walked and talked, just the two of us.

I told the man he could eat from all the trees of the garden, except one.

There was a tree in the beautiful garden called the tree of the knowledge of good and evil; that tree was forbidden.

I warned Adam that if he ever ate of the tree that he would surely die (Gen. 2:16–17).

I also created wonderful animals for Adam's pleasure. All of the animals were friendly. Sheep could pasture alongside wolves in complete safety.

Harm and death did not exist on earth. My earth was truly a magnificent paradise, stunning in all its wonder and glory from sunrise to sunset. Adam was given authority to oversee the garden and give names to all the marvelous animals of the earth.

After observing Adam for a while, I decided it was not good for him to be alone. Causing Adam to fall into a deep sleep, I removed a rib from his side and from this rib I formed a mate and partner for him called woman.

Eve is the name that Adam would give her. *Eve* means "mother of all the living" (Gen. 3:20). The first woman was very beautiful and created in such a way that she and Adam would complement each other physically and emotionally, in perfect intimacy.

They were both wonderfully made.

Adam awoke and upon seeing Eve, he immediately exclaimed "bone of my bones, and flesh of my flesh" (Gen. 2:22–23).

Their lives were full of love, beauty, peace, and harmony. I provided everything they would ever need. Now with My intimate fellowship and a perfectly designed and loving mate, if Adam so desired, he could be completely satisfied. He would never have to be lonely. The garden was truly bliss. It was a serene and peaceful paradise.

They had everything they wanted and needed. They were happy and content, living securely under My personal loving care.

Adam and Eve loved each other. I loved them both. *Everything was good.*

The Deception

In the eternal past, long before I created man and the garden, I had created other beings called angels. One who was especially beautiful served in My heavenly kingdom. His name was Satan and he was not satisfied with his status in heaven. Satan chose to rebel against Me, taking a third of the angels in heaven with him. (Ezek. 28:11–19).

I cast Satan, and his angels, who are called demons and fallen angels, down to earth to await judgement. Satan had become totally evil (Isa. 14:12–15).

It wasn't long until Satan came into the beautiful garden to entice My precious new creations to join in his rebellion.

He approached Adam and Eve as they were exploring the garden one day. Resting near the forbidden tree, they were unaware that evil was lurking nearby.

Appearing as an alluring serpent, Satan calmly said to Eve, "It looks good, doesn't it? Go ahead and eat. It's not really forbidden; just eat, eat the fruit on that tree. You won't die," he told her, "but rather you will become just like God" (Gen. 3:5).

The Invitation is Rejected

Eve, tempted by Satan, saw that the fruit was beautiful. She ate the fruit, and then gave some to Adam who also ate. In rebelling against Me, their eyes were opened to the knowledge of good and evil. Man's innocence was forever lost.

In a single tragic moment, sin and death began to invade the earth, bringing with it all of Satan's horrors, crimes, wars, lies, and perversions that humankind would face from that one single moment until this very day. This event would later be recorded as the Fall of Man.

By eating of the forbidden fruit, Adam and Eve brought themselves and their descendants under Satan's eternal curse and judgement.

Then My children, realizing what they had done, fearfully tried to hide from Me. Their peace and joy quickly began to disappear. They had separated themselves from Me, their Father, Maker, and Protector (Gen. 3:8).

I sensed the emptiness filling their hearts. No longer would the first man and woman naturally enjoy the comfort and blessings of My intimate presence in their lives. I, their Father and Creator, could no longer walk with them, because I am Holy, and holiness and evil cannot co-exist.

Peace was gone.

Evil began to shroud the entire earth as evidenced when Eve later bore children who brought murder into the world, with one son, Cain, killing the other son, Abel (Gen. 4:8).

Expelled from the garden, from that time on, Adam and Eve and all of humanity would live and eat by the sweat of their brow (Gen. 3:19).

The Invitation to Noah

As humanity multiplied upon the earth; violence and corruption spread. People used their freedom of choice to kill and destroy. I observed how their very thoughts were becoming continually evil (Gen. 6:5). Good and perfect things I had created were being perverted by evil men and women. All the people on the earth had corrupted their ways (Gen. 6:12).

Instead of loving and caring for each other, mankind began to rape and murder and steal. I was grieved deep in My heart that I had created mankind (Gen. 6:6). *Man chose evil, evil being the human's misuse of My good creation.* I would now send a great flood of water to cover the earth and cleanse the creation of their evil. All humanity would be destroyed, except one family.

Noah, a righteous descendant of Adam's third son Seth found favor in My eyes. I would save Noah and his family from the coming flood. Speaking to Noah, I warned him of this coming peril. A mighty boat was built to save his family and two, male and female, of every kind of animal of the earth and bird of the air. This evil generation would be erased from the earth. Life could begin new again after the flood.

Soon the waters receded and the earth was purified. I gave Noah and his family instructions much like I had given Adam, "Be fruitful and multiply and replenish the earth." I set a sign, a magnificent rainbow in the clouds, and I told Noah the rainbow would represent an everlasting covenant between Me and the earth and all living creatures of every kind. I made a promise to Noah and his family that no matter how corrupt humanity might become, I would never again use flood waters to destroy all life from the earth, and the rainbow would serve as a reminder of this promise (Gen. 9:11–17).

II

THE PREPARATION

An ancient heavenly truth held a hidden mystery. Unknown to all, there was a way to save humankind from the eternal consequence of their disobedience.

Long ago, outside the annals of space and time, I had prepared a way of salvation, a plan of deliverance should my human creation use their freedom of choice unwisely.

From the time of the fall, day after day, humankind would go on living in rebellion against me. My love, however, is greater than any human's rebellion.

One day in the distant future, at a time known only to Me, I would send a Redeemer to free all humanity from this curse.

Nations, Prophets, and Kings

Circa 2000 BC

Looking back and forth upon the entire earth I had created, I searched for someone who would be faithful, one would be set aside for My purpose. I would raise up a people whom I could call My own, from which the Redeemer would one day come.

I found such a man. His name was Abram. I called him *Abraham*, which means "father of many nations."

To My servant Abraham, who was an older child-less man, I promised that from his family I would make a mighty nation whose peoples would be more numerous than the stars in the sky (Gen. 26:4).

While Abraham believed and trusted in me, most of the world increased in rebellion against Me. Creating futile false gods, they carved images out of stone and wood and began worshipping these detestable, powerless idols.

Prophets were raised up who would testify on My behalf to the truth of who I was and how My people should live rightly before Me.

Circa 1500 BC

Another faithful servant was chosen; his name was Moses. I allowed Moses to work mighty wonders and miracles before the powerful pharaoh of Egypt and other kings of the earth (Exod. 7–12). I gave ten simple commandments to this prophet to teach My children how to live before Me.

Still my human creation continued in their rebellion. When their stone and wood gods failed to respond to their prayers, in frustration they melted gold and fashioned it into a calf and bowed down to worship the false god they had created (Exod. 32). They had chosen to worship the creature rather than the Creator.

Circa 1000 BC

I continued to search the earth for children who would be faithful to Me, I observed a shepherd boy named David valiantly protecting his sheep against the wild beasts of the night.

In the darkness, while quietly gazing at the stars, he would write beautiful songs and play them to Me on his harp. I listened. I loved him.

I took this shepherd boy and made him the mighty king of all Israel (2 Sam. 5). It was I who caused his single stone to fell the giant Goliath. When his nation was surrounded by hostile forces, it was I who won the battles. It was I who gave mighty King David wealth and prestige. It was I who gave him deep love and passion and inspiration. This beloved child was truly a man after My own heart (1 Sam. 13:14).

I would have given him anything he desired. Still it was not enough. Even as Adam and Eve had chosen to rebel, David took a married woman named Bathsheba and had her husband killed (2 Sam. 11). Even this great shepherd king, whom I especially loved, decided that he, too, wanted to taste forbidden fruit. *The sin of the garden had become the plague of all humanity.*

Circa 800 BC

Many messengers I now raised up to prophesy of the coming King and Redeemer who, through His suffering and dying, would pay for the sins of all mankind. I chose Isaiah, along with the prophets Elijah, Jeremiah, Ezekiel, Daniel, and many others to speak on My behalf to a world which, because of its sin, had long been separated from Me. However, My rebellious children would not listen.

Circa 400 BC

I, the Lord and God, Creator of the heavens and the earth and all that is within them, withheld My voice, no longer speaking through My prophets.

For four hundred years . . .

Silent . . .

Then . . . the time had come.

III

THE RESTORATION

Circa 1 AD

I had revealed through ancient historical writers and prophecies, there was One with Me in heaven who would come down to the earth in the form of a child (Isa. 7:14).

He would be born of a young virgin, a great grand descendant of Eve who had found favor in My eyes, a righteous young woman named Mary. Mary's conception would not be by man, rather by My Holy Spirit. My followers would later call this the Virgin Birth (Luke 1:30–35).

To this Son of Mine, I would give power to redeem Adam and Eve from their sin in the garden and all the descendants of the earth from Satan's grasp, freeing them also from their own wickedness and sins (John 1:12; Eph. 1:7).

This Son would bring man back into right relationship with Me, in this life, and forever in My heavenly kingdom (Luke 12:32).

Jesus the Christ is the name by which He, the Redeemer, would be known; the only begotten Son of God (Luke 1:31).

The arrival of Jesus on earth brought wondrous joy. Observers from foreign lands, aware of the prophecies concerning the time and place of My Son's birth, traveled a great distance just to worship Him with gifts of gold, frankincense, and myrrh (Matt. 2:11).

The celebration of this event would become known as Christmas. Future generations would greatly rejoice knowing that His birth and mission would bring forth the salvation of all humanity.

The timeline of world history would be ordered around His birth. The calendar of all past and future world events would be dated BC (Before Christ), and AD (*Anno Domini* which means "in the year of our Lord Jesus Christ").

My only begotten Son loved people with a love the world had never known.

With My anointing, at age thirty, He began working miraculous signs and wonders. He brought blessings and deliverance, healing and hope, everywhere He went.

He had come to set people free.

The Redeemer

Circa 30 AD

Since Adam and Eve's rebellion against Me, the earth had become terribly infected with diseases and evils. So I sent not only a Savior, but a miracle-working physician who revealed My love and power to heal and restore all humanity.

This Healer touched the deformed faces of lepers that no one would dare to come near, miraculously cleansing them. He gave sight to the blind who had never seen the glorious light of day. He told the lame who had never stood to stand up and walk (John 5:8).

He raised dead people up and gave them life (Luke 7:14). He forgave people of their sins. He rescued a prostitute who was about to be killed—saving, healing, and forgiving her (John 8:7–11).

He declared to the crowds "I am the way and the truth and the life. No one comes to the Father except through Me" (John 14:6).

My Son represented to the people what I was like. If they saw Him, they were seeing Me. Truly, love had come down from heaven in the form of a living man (John 1:14).

The Mystery

Jesus, though sent from heaven and fully divine, was fully human. He was tempted and tormented like every man and woman, yet He never sinned (Heb. 4:15).

Jesus had become flesh, living among the people, loving everyone. The great-grand descendants of

Adam and Eve could see in Jesus what I, their Father, was like and how I unconditionally loved them (John 14:9–11).

Angels had been given charge over Jesus lest He so much as dash His foot against a stone, however Satan was determined to destroy My Son (Ps. 91:11–12).

It was not for Satan to know what the true outcome of killing the Son of God would be. This was a great mystery.

The mystery was this: for humanity to be forgiven and reconciled to Me, a great price had to be paid for the sins of the world, committed throughout all time, from the fall of humanity in the garden to the future end of this present world (1 John 2:2).

Only holy, pure, and sinless blood could purchase My creation back and restore them to a right relationship with Me (Heb. 9:22). Life was in the blood. Redemption was in the blood.

The Ransom

For many centuries, the ritual blood sacrifice of perfect spotless lambs and other animals had been part of the fallen world. These bloody sacrifices were offered regularly as part of human worship in an effort to displace guilt and obtain transitory forgiveness for sin. My perfect and sinless Son would offer

Himself as the eternal sacrifice, forever ending this ancient practice. Jesus would become the sacrificial Lamb (Heb. 9:11–27).

The price for the rebellion was beyond human understanding or attainment. To break the curse of humanity, Jesus would have to live a perfect and sinless life and then allow Himself to be killed (John 10:18).

If the blood of My innocent and perfect Son, the promised Redeemer Jesus, would spill on the earth from which Adam was made, it would pay for the sin of the world, breaking the curse which began in the garden and forever set people free.

As the one man, Adam, had brought sin into the world, the one Man, Jesus, would conquer the world of sin (Rom. 5:19).

The Blood

Circa 33 AD

On the day of his prophesied betrayal, Jesus was charged with proclaiming to be the "Son of God." He had done no wrong, broken no laws, and was declared innocent by the Roman authorities. Pilate, the Roman governor, standing before Jesus' accusers took water and washed his hands declaring that he was free of this innocent man's blood (Matt. 27:24).

Still, Jesus was condemned to die the agonizing death of being nailed alive to a wooden cross.

My beloved Son, at the young age of thirty-three, allowed Satan and his demons, working through the hearts and minds of evil, jealous men, to torture and kill Him.

Powerful angelic beings would have intervened on My Son's behalf, but Jesus did not call upon them. For the sake of all humanity, He chose to drink the bitter cup of suffering. He was beaten unmercifully and beyond recognition, just as ancient prophecies had predicted (Isa. 52:14).

Jesus willingly endured the shame and terrible pain "for the joy set before Him" (Heb. 12:2). That joy was the knowledge that by giving His life, He would set all of humanity free, forever!

On this day in the ancient city of Jerusalem, Jesus was declared innocent, yet unjustly condemned. In unspeakable pain and agony, He was nailed to a wooden Roman cross, His innocent blood spilled on the ground as people shouted insults at Him. In His last breaths, Jesus, My precious Son, cried out, "It is finished!" (John 19:30).

Humanity was saved! All people were set free! Satan was defeated (Col. 2:14–15).

He was faithful to the very end. People called it the Crucifixion of Christ.

The sun and sky turned to darkness and the earth shook.

Inside the temple in Jerusalem there hung a curtain. This curtain represented an impenetrable veil signifying sinful humanity's inability to stand in My holy presence—I ripped it apart from top to bottom. Humanity was no longer separated from Me. All people everywhere could now come to Me boldly, in confidence and without fear. The pure blood debt for human sin was now satisfied by the death of My only begotten Son.

A Roman soldier who was given duty to stand guard at Jesus' execution, seeing what was taking place, shouted, "Surely He was the Son of God!" (Matt. 27:45–54).

The Redemption

My precious Son's body was removed from the cross and placed in a borrowed tomb.

On the third day, I sent an angel down from heaven to roll back the stone from the tomb. The angel's appearance was like lightning; his clothes were white as snow.

The Roman soldiers sent to guard the tomb saw this radiant angel. Filled with fear, they fell shaking to the ground and became as dead men (Matt. 28:2–4).

Later Jesus' accusers paid the Roman soldiers a large sum of money to keep them silent concerning what they had seen, telling them all to say that His disciples had stolen His body. This became the first of many attempts to deny the resurrection (Matt. 28:12–15).

On this, the third day, Jesus rose from the grave. I would not allow the body of My Son to see decay (Ps. 16:10).

His tomb lay empty (Luke 24:1–6).

My Son had conquered sin and death with His pure holy blood, victorious in the most important battle in all of history (Col. 1:20).

His followers would later come to celebrate this day. They would call it Easter or the Resurrection of Christ.

"Where, O death, is your victory? Where, O death, is your sting?" My prophets had declared! (1 Cor. 15:55).

It is only Jesus' pure and precious blood that saves humanity.

After rising from the dead, My Son appeared to many of His followers.

Witnesses of His resurrection trembled with fear upon seeing Him, others wept with great joy. Jesus allowed one who doubted to touch the wounds in His hands and feet (John 20:27).

He shared meals with His followers and explained to them how, through His death, suffering, and resurrection, they were now reunited back to Me as was predicted by Moses and the prophets (Luke 24:44).

Before ascending into heaven to be with Me, Jesus spent forty days with His followers and said to them, "All authority in heaven and on earth has been given to Me. Therefore go and make disciples of all nations, baptizing them in the name of the Father and of the Son and of the Holy Spirit, and teaching them to obey everything I have commanded you. And surely I am with you always, to the very end of the age" (1 Cor. 15:6; Matt. 28:18–20).

The New Invitation

Jesus' atoning death wondrously reunited humanity back to Me. However, those who reject or disregard His sacrifice will surely continue down the worldly path with Satan and his demons into the fires of hell. Those individuals will be separated from Me for all eternity (Mark 16:16; Rev. 20:15).

Hell was not created for man but for Satan and his rebellious demons. It is not My desire for anyone to perish. I deeply desire for all people everywhere to come to repentance (2 Pet. 2:4; 3:9).

I am not a respecter of persons. I care not if one has great wealth, prominence, or political influence in this earthly world, for "what good is it for a man to gain the whole world, yet forfeit his soul?" (Mark 8:36).

One day, each person will individually stand exposed before Me. The rich, the powerful, the weak, the poor. Any who have received Jesus will be welcomed into My Kingdom. Those who have rejected or disregarded My Son surely will not.

My anointed One, Jesus the Christ, broke Satan's curse, giving *every* human being a second chance—heaven or hell?

IV

THE ULTIMATE TRUTH

For two millennia, My followers have proclaimed this truth over the entire earth.

This is the true story of who you are, why you are here, and what's going to become of you.

My children, please understand this absolute reality: when your body dies, your eternal soul lives forever (Rev. 20:12–13).

One day, each of you will stand alone before Me (Heb. 4:13). If you have received forgiveness of your sins by intentionally humbling yourself and accepting My Son as your Lord and Savior, I will welcome you into My arms and into the wonderful kingdom of heaven (Rev. 21:3–7).

You are the joy that My Son saw when He allowed Himself to be tortured to death.

Throughout the centuries, untold numbers have chosen to love and follow Jesus. They are My Son's reward.

He is the *only* way. I, the Creator of the heavens and the earth, established Him, and Him alone.

"No one comes to the Father except through Me," My Son declared (John 14:6).

There is no other way to heaven. I made it so simple a child can understand.

Jesus is the only True King!

Jesus is your only hope.

I am offering you, My treasured children, an eternal home with Me. Always remember, like Adam and Eve, I will not violate your free will or your ability to choose (Matt. 23:37).

While you live, you can choose. When you die your choice becomes locked into eternity. Never again will there be an opportunity to choose (Luke 16:19–25).

Hell is real! All men and women who refuse to accept the authority of the curse-breaking blood sacrifice of Jesus Christ will continue on into the place of eternal desolation and separation from Me (Rev. 20:14–15).

Heaven is real! There will be a new heaven and a new earth. Anyone, regardless of family heritage or ancestry, wealth or poverty, intelligence or abilities, who will simply receive the free gift of Jesus Christ will be welcomed into this magnificent paradise—a place of limitless beauty, joy, peace, and love (Rev. 21:10–27).

The Infinite Truth

There are only two destinations.

One is wonderful. One unthinkable.

"For wide is the gate and broad is the road that leads to destruction, and many enter through it. But small is the gate and narrow the road that leads to life, and only a few find it" (Matt. 7:13–14).

My Word declares that all have sinned and fallen short of My glory, and that the wages of your sin is death (Rom. 3:23; 6:23).

The truth is, every sin you have ever committed can be washed clean by the precious blood of My Son Jesus (Rom. 8:1; Eph. 1:7).

There is freedom in the blood of Jesus if you trust in Him and accept His sacrifice as your own.

Freedom from eternal death and damnation. Freedom from the bondage of sin. Freedom from the fear of death. Freedom from depression. Freedom from every addiction. Freedom from bitterness and loneliness, anger, and hopelessness.

This wonderful freedom will bring to you the peace that passes all understanding. I, your Heavenly Father and your God, will wipe away every tear from your eye (Phil. 4:7; Rev. 21:4).

I AM your Creator and Father, there is nothing in this material world that will ever satisfy you. Only a loving relationship with Me can bring the perfect peace and joy that totally satisfies the deepest longing of your soul.

Know this: I who AM eternal see the precious innocent child you once were; I also can foresee the joy and victory your life will become when you trust and follow Me!

Please do not choose the path of rebellion that leads to eternal death; rather, choose the path of obedience prepared by Jesus which leads to eternal peace, love, and joy.

My precious Son, Jesus the Messiah, allowed Himself to be tortured to death for your sins so you can live forever with Me in glory!

When you die in Christ, I will give you a new, wonderful, glorified body that will never decay, or know pain or suffering.

What Security! What Safety! What Love! What Freedom! What Victory! What a glorious future! (Rev. 21).

Jesus calls you His friend. He loves you. *I love you!* (John 15:14).

I AM Who I AM

I AM the Ancient of Days.
I know of your pain and brokenness.
I AM the One Who Is, Who Was, and Who Is to Come.
I know your dreams and desires.
I AM the Alpha and the Omega (Rev. 1:8).

Nothing is hidden from Me. I know all you have been through, your secret thoughts, and your deepest longings. I, who created you, know your greatest achievements and your humiliating shame. I am not angry with you.

I know your name. I even know how many hairs are on your head (Luke 12:7).

Please realize, only a personal relationship with Me will satisfy your heart and soul.

Loneliness, fear, and emptiness can be transformed into an overflowing fullness of love and joy if you would only trust in Me.

Jesus is saying, "Come to me, all you who are weary and burdened and I will give you rest" (Matt. 11:28).

Listen carefully.

It is My Son, Jesus, who will knock at the door of your heart.

Find a quiet place and invite Him in.

He is anticipating the sound of your voice.

He is not angry with you.

Remember you are the joy He saw as He was dying on the cross.

He forgives you—of even your most vile and shameful sins.

He invites you to receive this forgiveness.

He purchased you with a great price, proving His love for you.

He is the Name above all names.

He is the Lord of Lords.

He is the King of Kings.

You are of immeasurable value to Him.

He is *your* Lord and Savior.

He is waiting . . . for *you*.

THE REASON FOR CHRIST

Christ's sacrifice on the cross reunited
man to God forever.
"For God sent not His Son into the world
to condemn the world; but that the world
through Him might be saved."
—JOHN 3:17 KJV

Christ's blood sacrifice freed mankind
from eternal condemnation.
"I tell you the truth, whoever hears My word and
believes Him who sent Me has eternal
life and will not be condemned; he has
crossed over from death to life."
—JOHN 5:24

Christ proved once and forever God's
never ending Love for mankind.
"For God so loved the world, that He gave
His only begotten Son, that whosoever believeth
in Him should not perish, but
have everlasting life."
—JOHN 3:16 KJV

Recognizing Christ

You must accept that you have sinned against God.
"For all have sinned and
fall short of the glory of God."
—Romans 3:23

Know that the consequence of sin is eternal death.
"For the wages of sin is death, but the gift of God
is eternal life in Christ Jesus our Lord."
—Romans 6:23

Recognize that Jesus paid for all your sins.
"But God demonstrates His own love for us in
this: While we were still sinners,
Christ died for us."
—Romans 5:8

Receive forgiveness by trusting in Jesus Christ.
"That if you confess with your mouth, 'Jesus is
Lord,' and believe in your heart that God raised
Him from the dead, you will be saved."
—Romans 10:9

INVITATION OF CHRIST

"EVERYONE WHO CALLS ON THE NAME
OF THE LORD WILL BE SAVED."
—ROMANS 10:13

These are the words of Jesus:

"If anyone is thirsty, let him
come to Me and drink."
—JOHN 7:37

"Ask and it will be given to you;
seek and you will find;
knock and the door will be opened to you."
—LUKE 11:9

"I am the light of the world.
Whoever follows me will never walk in darkness,
but will have the light of life."
—JOHN 8:12

RECEIVING CHRIST

The prayer on the following page is based on truth found in the Holy Scriptures. New believers have long used these words, or similar ones, to acknowledge a new-found belief in Jesus Christ. Saying this prayer may be the most important thing you will ever do.

If you believe, simply verbalize to God what is happening in your heart. If you have already received Christ and want to reaffirm with thanksgiving your commitment to Him, this prayer is good for that purpose as well.

If you so desire, find a quiet place and pray this prayer. It is a prayer to ask forgiveness of sins and invite Jesus Christ into your life. It is commonly called the Sinners Prayer.

We refer to it as the Salvation Prayer.

SALVATION PRAYER

Dear Lord Jesus,

I believe You are the Son of God and that You died on the cross for my sins. I believe You rose on the third day and all power in the heavens and on the earth has been given to You by God the Father.

Please come into my heart, take control of my life, and live inside of me. Please forgive me of my sins. Cast them as far as the East is from the West and remember them no more. Fill me with Your Holy Spirit and grant that I may live with You in the glorious kingdom of heaven forever and ever. Be my Lord and Savior.

From this day forward and forever more, I belong to You, Lord Jesus!

Amen

DECLARATION

I, _____, have
received Jesus Christ as my Lord and Savior.

On or about this date:

_____

In the province, city, or town of:

_____

Signed:

_____

Witness:

_____

LIVING FOR ETERNITY

LIVING FOR CHRIST

Proclamation

If you have become a believer in Jesus Christ, *let others know!* This strengthens your faith and gives others an opportunity to become believers.

"Whoever acknowledges Me before men, I will also acknowledge him before My Father in heaven," Jesus declared (Matt. 10:32).

Prayer

Thank God for His goodness. Celebrate your eternal salvation. God dwells in the praises of His people. Telling the Lord that you love Him is a great way to start the day. Simply put, prayer is talking to God. Pray out loud or pray quietly in your heart. God will hear you. Pray as often as you like. Stop and listen. The Bible declares that the prayers of the saints are a sweet fragrance to the Lord.

"In everything, by prayer and petition, with thanksgiving, present your requests to God. And the peace of God, which transcends all understanding, will guard your hearts and your minds in Christ Jesus" (Phil. 4:6–7).

Scripture

The Bible is life! It breathes! It will teach you how to live an abundant and victorious life!

Treasure the Word. Read the New Testament first, then the Old. Find out why people were willing to be persecuted just for the privilege of reading the "Book of Books."

In 1536 English linguist William Tyndale (1494–1536) was strangled and his body burned at the stake after translating much of the Bible into modern English.

Many saints were martyred and still, daily, others are being martyred around the world for the opportunity to simply read the Bible in their own language.

Get to know who God is, how much He loves you, and what He expects from you. Reading the Word can cleanse ungodly thoughts in your mind and can replace them with godly thoughts. God makes provision for answers to your questions in the Bible.

Daily reading of God's Word can give you victory in all areas of your life.

"Do not conform any longer to the pattern of this world, but be transformed by the renewing of your mind" (Rom. 12:2).

Baptism

Since the time of the apostles, all new believers have been baptized. Receiving Christ was soon followed by water baptism as was commanded by Jesus in Mark 16:15–16; by Peter in Acts 2:38 and Acts 10:47; demonstrated by Philip in Acts 8:36; and by Paul in Acts 19:4–5.

You can be baptized by any minister of the gospel; a faithful disciple, preacher, pastor, or priest.

Holy Spirit

Jesus has given His Holy Spirit to comfort, empower, and guide us (John 14:15–18).

Pray to receive the fullness of the Holy Spirit, and then believe you have received it.

The Holy Spirit wants to give you peace in any situation. He will also give you an increasing disdain for sin.

Remember, if you do stumble and sin, confess it immediately to the Lord who is faithful to forgive you.

"If we confess our sins, He is faithful and just and will forgive us our sins and purify us from all unrighteousness" (1 John 1:9).

Ask the Lord for the filling of His Holy Spirit while you pray the Sinner's Prayer or while you are being baptized or just ask the Lord to fill you now. *The Holy Spirit desires to continually fill you and empower you to live a deep and meaningful Christian life.*

The Holy Spirit is called a Helper and a Comforter, who gives spiritual gifts which will equip you for service to God in His kingdom on this earth. These wonderful spiritual gifts are referenced in 1 Corinthians 12:27–31.

Preparation

Never forget, Satan is the arch enemy of all saints, and you must be aware and knowledgeable in order not to fall for his tricks or deceptions. The Bible proclaims that there is no truth in him and that he is a "liar and the father of lies" (John 8:44). Satan has come to kill, steal, and destroy. He is a roaring lion seeking whomever he may devour (1 Pet. 5:8). However, if you renew your mind with the reading of God's Word, prayer, fellowship, and obedience to God, *Satan will never maintain power over you.* In Ephesians, the Bible tells us: "For our struggle is not against flesh and blood, but against the rulers . . . of this dark world and against the spiritual forces of evil in the heavenly realms. Therefore put on the full armor of God, so that when the day of evil comes, you may be able to stand your ground" (Eph. 6:12–13).

Fellowship

Find a church that recognizes the deity of Christ, that He is the only way to heaven and there is no other way. Find a place where the Bible is read and treasured above all books. Find a community where there is a wonderful, adoring worship of God and a great joy and passion for following Christ.

Get involved in smaller fellowships such as Bible studies or home groups as these will help you to grow and be accountable to other believers.

A hot coal pulled from the fire will quickly die. Don't be a loner. *Intentionally seek godly friends.* If you cannot find a suitable faith community, fast and pray, then start a home fellowship and invite your friends and family. "Let us not give up meeting together" (Heb. 10:25).

Holy Communion

All Christian churches practice the memorial of Holy Communion. It is wonderful to partake of the bread, or body of Christ, and the wine, or blood of Christ. *It is a powerful opportunity to meditate on the unfathomable love of the King of Kings.* "While they were eating, Jesus took bread, gave thanks and broke it, and gave it to his disciples, saying, 'Take it; this is My body.' Then He took the cup, gave thanks and offered it to them, and they all drank from it. 'This is My blood of the covenant, which is poured out for many,' He said to them. 'I tell you the truth, I will not drink again of the fruit of the vine until that day when I drink it anew in the kingdom of God'" (Mark 14:22–24).

Love

God is love. When you receive Jesus you can become a conduit of His love enabling you to love others, even the unlovable.

Your life can become an endless flowing fountain of true love, flowing from God to be shared with others. His love is so much greater than human or physical love.

His love can soften the hardest heart, heal the deepest wounds, and comfort the loneliest depths of one's soul. His love is patient; it is kind. It does not envy nor does it boast. It is not proud nor rude nor self-seeking. His love is not easily angered and keeps no record of wrongs. His love does not delight in evil but rejoices with the truth. His love always protects, always hopes, and always perseveres. His love never fails (1 Cor. 13).

Jesus said, "Greater love has no one than this, that he lay down his life for his friends" (John 15:13).

He did this for His friends—*you and me.*

The Ten Commandments

The shed blood of Christ beautifully and wondrously pays the penalty for all who have ever broken God's commandments; however, these unchanging laws of God represent the high standard to which we are to aspire, even to this very day.

The Ten Commandments are actually ten *freedoms* that enable us to live our lives faithfully, abundantly, and with great joy. *They were written by God's own hand,* in an effort to show sinful man the proper way to live according to His universal laws. Jesus said "I have not come to abolish [the Law] but to fulfill [the Law]" (Matt. 5:17).

Forgiveness of sin and payment for mankind's breaking of the law was Jesus' magnificent gift to all mankind. Shortly before He allowed His cleansing blood to be spilled upon the ground that Adam was made from He said this:

"'Love the LORD your God with all your heart and with all your soul and with all your mind.' This is the first and greatest commandment. And the second is like it: 'Love your neighbor as yourself.' All the Law and the Prophets hang on these two commandments" (Matt. 22:37–40). It is, and always was, all about love.

THE TEN COMMANDMENTS

1. You shall have no other gods before Me.

2. You shall not make for yourself an idol in the form of anything in heaven above or on the earth beneath.

3. You shall not misuse the name of the LORD your God.

4. Remember the Sabbath day by keeping it holy.

5. Honor your father and your mother.

6. You shall not murder.

7. You shall not commit adultery.

8. You shall not steal.

9. You shall not give false testimony against your neighbor.

10. You shall not covet.

EXODUS 20

FREEDOM IN CHRIST

IF THE SON SETS YOU FREE,
YOU WILL BE FREE INDEED.
—John 8:36

When you are filled with the Holy Spirit and the knowledge of God's word, you can become increasingly free from the compulsion to sin. (John 8:31–32). This is true freedom.

In Christ you can be set free from *pride, anger, greed, addictions, idolatry, witchcraft, lust of the flesh, sexual immorality, malice, covetousness, vain desires, hatred, selfishness, blasphemy, unbelief, envy, filthy communication, demonic influences,* and all of the foolish habits that destroy and make life miserable (Gal. 5:19–21). Freedom from these afflictions will be realized in your life more and more as you diligently seek God.

Growing faith in Christ brings *love, peace, joy, happiness, kindness, self control, goodness, righteousness, truth, holiness, sound mind, pure thoughts, clear thinking, meekness, temperance, gentleness, goodness, faith,* and all of the habits that make life beautiful for you and those around you (Gal. 5:22–23).

The Return of Christ

No one knows about that day or hour, not even the angels in heaven, nor the Son, but only the Father. Be on guard! Be alert! (Mark 13:32–33).

Mystery surrounds the prophecies of Christ's second coming, an event that will end life as it is now known on this earth. Christ's return will usher in a new heavenly reign (Rev. 21:1). This epic event has been the source of much speculation for centuries.

The Bible states in the last days people will become: "lovers of themselves, lovers of money, boastful, proud, abusive, disobedient to their parents, ungrateful, unholy, without love, unforgiving, slanderous, without self-control, brutal, not lovers of the good, treacherous, rash, conceited, lovers of pleasure rather than lovers of God . . . men of depraved minds" (2 Tim. 3:2–8).

Jesus says, "Watch out that no one deceives you. Many will come in My name, claiming, 'I am he,' and will deceive many. When you hear of wars and rumors of wars, do not be alarmed. Such things must happen, but the end is still to come. Nation will rise against nation, and kingdom against kingdom. There will be earthquakes in various places and famines. These are the beginnings of birth pains" (Mark 13:5–8).

Jesus goes on to describe a time of great distress coming upon the earth right before He returns and states, "at that time men will see the Son of Man coming in clouds with great power and glory" (Mark 13:26).

Whether one lives to see Christ's return, or dies and then stands before Him, "keep watch, because you do not know on what day your Lord will come" (Matt. 24:42). We have been instructed to live our lives as though He were to return at any moment.

Each generation has longed to see Jesus' return. Be encouraged. Be faithful. Live expectantly, lest you find yourself unprepared and miss the opportunity to unite with Christ in His heavenly kingdom.

TESTIMONY OF WITNESSES

Statesmen Speak about Jesus and the Bible

United States Presidents

"You do well to wish to learn our arts and ways of life, and above all, the religion of Jesus Christ."

—**George Washington** (1722–1799)
1st President of the United States
Speech to the Delaware Indian Chiefs, May 12, 1779

"The Bible is the best book in the world." "Our constitution was made only for a moral and religious people. It is wholly inadequate to the government of any other."

—**John Adams** (1735–1826)
2nd President of the United States
Letter to Thomas Jefferson, December 25, 1813;
Speech to military officers, October 11, 1798

"I hold the precepts of Jesus as delivered by Himself, to be the most pure, benevolent, and sublime which have ever been preached to man."

—**Thomas Jefferson** (1743–1826)
3rd President of the United States
Letter to Jared Sparks, November 4, 1820

"A watchful eye must be kept on ourselves lest while we are building ideal monuments of Renown and Bliss here we neglect to have our names enrolled in the Annals of Heaven."

—James Madison (1751–1836)
4TH PRESIDENT OF THE UNITED STATES
Letter to William Bradford, November 9, 1772

"For these blessings we owe to Almighty God, from whom we derive them."

—James Monroe (1758–1831)
5TH PRESIDENT OF THE UNITED STATES
Eighth annual address to Congress, December 7, 1824

"The Sermon on the Mount commands me to lay up for myself treasures, not upon earth, but in Heaven. My hopes of a future life are all founded upon the Gospel of Christ."

—John Quincy Adams (1767–1848)
6TH PRESIDENT OF THE UNITED STATES
Letter written from London, December 24, 1814

"That book [the Bible], sir, is the Rock upon which our republic rests." "The Bible is true. . . . Upon that sacred volume I rest my hope of eternal salvation, through the merits and blood of our blessed Lord and Saviour, Jesus Christ."

—Andrew Jackson (1767–1856)
7TH PRESIDENT OF THE UNITED STATES
Spoken in reference to the Bible, June 1, 1845;
First clause of Andrew Jackson's will

"The atonement of Jesus Christ is the only remedy and rest for my soul."

—**Martin Van Buren** (1782–1862)
<small>8TH PRESIDENT OF THE UNITED STATES</small>
Spoken during his last illness, 1860

"Those nations only are blessed whose God is the Lord." "In regard to this Great Book, I have but to say, . . . the Bible is the best gift God has given to man. All the good the Saviour gave to the world was communicated through this Book. But for this Book we could not know right from wrong."

—**Abraham Lincoln** (1809–1865)
<small>16TH PRESIDENT OF THE UNITED STATES</small>
Proclamation appointing a national fast day, March 30, 1863;
Acknowledging the gift of a Bible from African American
citizens of Baltimore, September 5, 1864

"Hold fast to the Bible as the sheet anchor of your liberties; write its precepts in your hearts, and practice them in your lives."

—**Ulysses S. Grant** (1822–1885)
<small>18TH PRESIDENT OF THE UNITED STATES</small>
Writing to the editor of the Sunday School Times,
June 6, 1876

"I am a firm believer in the Divine teachings, perfect example, and atoning sacrifice of Jesus Christ."

—**Rutherford B. Hayes** (1822–1893)
<small>19TH PRESIDENT OF THE UNITED STATES</small>

"Our faith teaches that there is no safer reliance than upon the God of our fathers, who has so singularly favored the American people in every national trial, and who will not forsake us so long as we obey His commandments and walk humbly in His footsteps."

—**William McKinley (1843–1901)**
25TH PRESIDENT OF THE UNITED STATES
Inaugural address March 4, 1897

"My great joy and glory is that, in occupying an exalted position in the nation, I am enabled, to preach the practical moralities of the Bible to my fellow-countrymen and to hold up Christ as the hope and Savior of the world."

—**Theodore Roosevelt (1858–1919)**
26TH PRESIDENT OF THE UNITED STATES

"The Bible . . . is the one supreme source of revelation of the meaning of life."

—**Woodrow Wilson (1856–1924)**
28TH PRESIDENT OF THE UNITED STATES
Spoken at a Denver rally in 1911

"I have always believed in the inspiration of the Holy Scriptures, whereby they have become the expression to man of the Word and will of God."

—**Warren G. Harding (1865–1923)**
29TH PRESIDENT OF THE UNITED STATES

"This civilization and this great complex, which we call American life, is [built] and can alone survive upon the translation into individual action of that fundamental philosophy announced by the Savior nineteen centuries ago."

—Herbert Hoover (1874–1964)
31ST PRESIDENT OF THE UNITED STATES
Radio address to the nation, October 18, 1931

"It is fitting that we give thanks with special fervor to our Heavenly Father. . . . That we may bear more earnest witness to our gratitude to Almighty God, I suggest a nationwide reading of the Holy Scriptures during the period from Thanksgiving Day to Christmas."

—Franklin D. Roosevelt (1882–1945)
32ND PRESIDENT OF THE UNITED STATES
Thanksgiving Day Proclamation, November 1, 1944

"Through Jesus Christ the world will be a better and a fairer place." "All our traditions have come from Moses at Sinai, and Jesus on the Mount." "The fundamental basis of our Bill of Rights comes from the teachings which we get from Exodus and St. Matthew, from Isaiah and St. Paul."

—Harry S. Truman (1884–1972)
33RD PRESIDENT OF THE UNITED STATES
National Christmas Tree Lighting, December 24, 1952;
Augustana Lutheran Church, June 7, 1950;
Attorney General's Law Enforcement Conference,
February 15, 1950

"Without God, there could be no American form of Government, nor an American way of life. Recognition of the Supreme Being is the first—the most basic—expression of Americanism. Thus the Founding Fathers saw it, and thus, with God's help, it will continue to be."

—Dwight D. Eisenhower (1890–1968)
34TH PRESIDENT OF THE UNITED STATES
American Legion, February 20, 1955

"The rights of man come not from the generosity of the state but from the hand of God."

—John F. Kennedy (1917–1963)
35TH PRESIDENT OF THE UNITED STATES
Inaugural address, January 20, 1961

"Within the covers of that single Book are all the answers to all the problems that face us today. . . . The Bible can touch our hearts, order our minds, refresh our souls." "And, by dying for us, Jesus showed how far our love should be ready to go: all the way."

—Ronald Reagan (1911–2004)
40TH PRESIDENT OF THE UNITED STATES
Address to National Religious Broadcasters, January 31, 1983;
Address to National Religious Broadcasters, January 30, 1984

"I commit to the dust, relying on the merits of Jesus Christ for the pardon of my sins."

—**Samuel Adams** (1722–1803)
American founding father and signer of
the Declaration of Independence; written in his will

"The Bible is worth all other books which have ever been printed."

—**Patrick Henry** (1736–1799)
American founding father, famous for
the quote: "Give me liberty or give me death."

"God Governs in the affairs of men. . . . We have been assured, sir, in the sacred writings, that 'except the Lord build the house, they labor in vain that build it.'"

—**Benjamin Franklin** (1706–1790)
American founding father,
printer, publisher, statesman, and inventor;
from the Constitutional Convention of 1787

"In forming and settling my belief relative to the doctrines of Christianity, I adopted no articles from creeds but such only as, on careful examination, I found to be confirmed by the Bible."

—**John Jay** (1745–1829)
President of the Continental Congress,
First Chief Justice of the U.S. Supreme Court

"Education is useless without the Bible." "The Bible was America's basic text book in all fields." "God's Word, contained in the Bible, has furnished all necessary rules to direct our conduct."

—Noah Webster (1758–1843)
Educator and author of Webster's Dictionary, *he was known as the "Schoolmaster of the Nation"*

"I fully accept it [the Bible] as the infallible Word of God, and receive its teachings as inspired by the Holy Spirit." "The Bible has never failed to give me light and strength."

—Robert E. Lee (1807–1870)
Commander of the Confederate Army of Northern Virginia in the American Civil War

"Believe me, sir, never a night goes by, be I ever so tired, but I read the Word of God before I go to bed."

—Gen. Douglas MacArthur (1880–1964)
Supreme Commander of the Allied Forces in the Pacific during World War II

"God will not reject a heart that's broken and sorry for sin. He's not waiting to condemn you, to judge you. He's waiting to kiss you and say 'I love you.'"

—Billy Graham (born 1918)
Pastor to the Presidents, preached live to over two hundred million people, considered the most admired person of the twentieth century

World Leaders

"That book [the Bible] accounts for the supremacy of England."

—**Queen Victoria (1819–1876)**
*Queen of England; said upon receiving
a Bible at her coronation, June 28, 1837*

"Alexander, Caesar, Charlemagne, and I have founded empires. But on what did we rest the creations of our genius? Upon force! Jesus Christ founded His empire upon love; and at this hour millions of men would die for Him."

—**Napoleon Bonaparte (1769–1821)**
*French General and Emperor of France;
discussion with Count de Montholon*

"Our Lord Jesus Christ, the Son of God, when faced with His terrible choice and lonely vigil, *chose* to lay down His life that our sins may be forgiven."

—**Margaret Thatcher (born 1925)**
*Prime Minister of the United Kingdom; in a speech
to the Church of Scotland General Assembly 1988*

"We rest with assurance upon 'the impregnable rock of Holy Scripture.'"

—**Sir Winston Churchill (1874–1965)**
*Prime Minister of the United Kingdom;
from his book* Amid These Storms

HISTORICAL, SCIENTIFIC,
AND
SOCIOLOGICAL EVIDENCE

The History and Science of the Bible

The Bible is the largest selling book in world history. It has been translated into more than twelve hundred languages with nearly thirty million copies distributed worldwide annually.

Written over fifteen hundred years, from 1400 BC to 100 AD, the Bible contains the only genealogy in history dating back to Adam in the garden.

The Bible contains more than three hundred specific prophecies concerning a coming Jewish Messiah that were all fulfilled by Christ.

The New Testament is unparalleled among historical writings, with more than thirteen thousand complete and partial manuscripts in Greek and other languages surviving antiquity. From 40 AD until 90 AD, Jesus' eye witnesses and followers wrote the books of the New Testament. The writers—Mark, John, Paul, Luke, Jude, Peter, Matthew, and James—quote from thirty-one of the Old Testament books.

The sixty-six books were written by more than forty authors from different walks of life including fishermen, shepherds, farmers, physicians, priests, prophets, and kings. Written on three continents, in three languages with absolute accuracy, and cohesion as inspired by the living God.

Since 1400 BC, faithful scribes dedicated their lives to the preservation of the Bible. Any error would require the entire scroll to be destroyed. The twentieth century discovery of the Dead Sea Scrolls confirmed the scribes' amazing accuracy in the recording of the Bible.

Archaeological and Scientific Evidence

Archaeological surveys continually affirm with surgical precision biblical accounts. From the unearthing of the world's oldest city, Jericho (1867, corroborating the biblical account), to discoveries like the "House of David" inscription stone (1994, attesting to King David's historical role), and the "Pontius Pilate" inscription stone (1961, affirming Pontius Pilate's governorship), verified accordingly by several ancient (non-biblical) historians—including Josephus, Pliny, and Tacitus. Archaeological revelations have served only to authenticate biblical chronology.

Individuals with scientific understanding have long recognized that the biblical writers could not have possibly understood the scientific truths about which they wrote without divine inspiration. Here are examples of scientific truths reflected in the Scriptures:

"[He] who is eight days old must be circumcised" (Gen. 17:12). Twentieth century science proved the eighth day is when the body's immune system peaks.

The Bible declared the earth to be circular, floating freely in space and the stars without number thousands of years before these truths were discovered by modern science (Job 26:7; Jer. 33:22).

The book of Leviticus describes healthy nutrition and proper food preparation for protection from disease, the spreading of germs and bacteria thousands of years before these practices were verified by science.

The Bible describes the sanitary practice of washing with running water (Lev. 15:13 KJV). Physicians routinely infected and caused accidental death to patients by washing in still-water basins until 1845 when an Austrian physician discovered this biblical truth.

These and many other fascinating sciences were revealed in the Bible thousands of years before being confirmed by the inventions of the microscope and telescope.

SCIENTISTS SPEAK ABOUT
JESUS AND THE BIBLE

"No sciences are better attested than the religion of the Bible." "I have a fundamental belief in the Bible as the Word of God, written by men who were inspired. I study the Bible daily."

—**Sir Isaac Newton (1642–1727)**
*Mathematician, physicist, inventor of calculus,
among the most influential scientists in history*

"God is going to reveal to us things He never revealed before if we put our hands in His. . . . Without God to draw aside the curtain I would be helpless."

—**George Washington Carver (1863–1943)**
*Botanist, educator, inventor, considered
the greatest African American scientist*

"The more I study nature, the more I stand amazed at the work of the Creator." "Science brings men nearer to God."

—**Louis Pasteur (1822–1895)**
*French chemist, considered the "Father of
Microbiology," developer of pasteurization*

"The nearer I approach to the end of my pilgrimage, the clearer is the evidence of the divine origin of the Bible."

—**Samuel Morse (1791–1872)**
Inventor of the telegraph

"Order is manifestly maintained in the universe . . . governed by the sovereign will of God." "After the knowledge of, and obedience to, the will of God, the next aim must be to know something of His attributes of wisdom, power, and goodness as evidenced by His handiwork."

—James Prescott Joule (1818–1889)
English physicist who described the First Law of
Thermodynamics—the Law of Conservation of Energy
(a unit of energy in physics is a "joule")

"I prayed to the most merciful Lord about my heart's great desire, and He gave me the spirit and the intelligence for the task. . . . It was the Lord who put into my mind (I could feel His hand upon me). . . . All who heard of my project rejected it with laughter, ridiculing me."

—Christopher Columbus (1401–1506)
Navigator, colonizer, and explorer; concerning
sailing around a world that many thought to be flat

"The Bible called the earth 'the round world,' yet for ages it was the most damnable heresy for Christian men to say that the world is round; and, finally, sailors circumnavigated the globe, and proved the Bible to be right."

—Matthew Fontaine Maury (1806–1873)
Astronomer, oceanographer, meteorologist;
considered the "Father of Oceanography";
he states that he discovered the "oceanic currents"
from Psalm 8:8 and "atmospheric circulation and
wind weight" from Ecclesiastes 1:6 and Job 28:25

"As a child I received instruction both in the Bible and in the Talmud. I am a Jew, but I am enthralled by the luminous figure of the Nazarene." "No one can read the Gospels without feeling the actual presence of Jesus. His personality pulsates in every word. No myth is filled with such life."

—**Albert Einstein (1879–1955)**
Theoretical physicist, discovered the "theory of relativity";
from a Saturday Evening Post *interview,*
"What Life Means to Einstein," October 26, 1929

"I see DNA, the information molecule of all living things, as God's language. . . . The God of the Bible is also the God of the genome. God can be found in the cathedral or in the laboratory. By investigating God's majestic and awesome creation, science can actually be a means of worship."

—**Dr. Francis Collins (born 1950)**
American physician, geneticist, author, director of the National Human Genome Research Institute, and referred to in Time *magazine as "The man who cracked the genome"*

"In this age of space flight, when we use the modern tools of science to advance into new regions of human activity, the Bible—this grandiose, stirring history of the gradual revelation and unfolding of the moral law—remains in every way an up-to-date book."

—**Wernher Von Braun (1912–1977)**
NASA director, considered the preeminent rocket engineer of the twentieth century

"My walk on the moon lasted for three days and was great, but putting my faith in Jesus as my Savior put me on an eternal walk that is even greater."

—Charles Duke (born 1935)
*Apollo 16 astronaut, youngest of only
twelve people to walk on the moon*

"The relation of geology, as well as astronomy, to the Bible, when both are well understood, is that of perfect harmony." "The Word and the works of God cannot conflict, and the more they are studied the more perfect will their harmony appear."

—Benjamin Silliman (1779–1864)
*Physicist, Yale professor, and founder of
the American Journal of Science and Arts*

"With regard to the origin of life, science . . . positively affirms creative power."

—Lord Kelvin [William Thomson] (1824–1907)
*Scottish physicist, creator of the Kelvin temperature scale
(absolute temperatures are given as "kelvins")*

"Jesus Christ. . . . Let me never be separated from Him. We keep hold of Him only by the ways taught in the Gospel. . . . Total submission to Jesus Christ."

—Blaise Pascal (1623–1662)
*Scientist, philosopher, and inventor; worked in physics,
hydrostatics, and vacuums; from a manuscript in his own
handwriting, dated November 23, 1654,
found in his coat at his death*

TESTIMONIES
OF THE DYING

ETERNAL DESTINY

The following pages contain the dying words of those who received Christ in life, those who denied Him, and those who begged for mercy in their final moments before the inevitable curtain of death closed in upon them.

In defeating Satan, with a love this world has never known, Jesus conquered sin and death making a way to eternal paradise for those who choose to follow Him. "He has also set eternity in the hearts of men" (Eccl. 3:11).

As Jesus declared in His divine revelation to John, "I am the Living One; I was dead, and behold I am alive for ever and ever! And I hold the keys of death and Hades" (Rev. 1:18).

"Man is destined to die once, and after that to face judgment" (Heb. 9:27). Such eternal judgment is for God alone to make. Take a moment and ponder the following statements as you consider your own eternal destiny.

DYING IN CHRIST

"I commit my soul to the mercy of God, through our Lord and Saviour Jesus Christ, and I exhort my dear children humbly to try and guide themselves by the teaching of the New Testament."

—**Charles Dickens** (1812–1870)
English novelist; written in his last will and testament

"My sufferings are as nothing compared with that which our blessed Redeemer endured upon the accursed Cross, that all might be saved who put their trust in Him. . . . I am my God's. I belong to Him."

—**Andrew Jackson** (1767–1845)
7th president of the United States of America; spoken moments before death June 8, 1845

"See in what peace a Christian can die."

—**Joseph Addison** (1672–1719)
English essayist, poet, and politician; spoken shortly before his death

"Lord Jesus, receive my spirit."

—**Thomas Cranmer** (1489–1556)
Archbishop of Canterbury; his final words as he was burned at the stake for faith in Christ

"I commend my soul into the hands of God my Creator, hoping and assuredly believing, through the only merits of Jesus Christ my Saviour, to be made partaker of life everlasting; and my body to the earth, whereof it is made."

—William Shakespeare (1564–1616)
English poet and playwright; words written in his will

"I am trusting Christ's death for me to take me to heaven."

—Mickey Mantle (1931–1995)
Baseball Hall of Fame athlete;
spoken just days before he died

"Jesus, I love you. Jesus, I love you."

—Mother Teresa (1910–1997)
Roman Catholic nun and missionary; her final words

"This is the end of earth, I am content."

—John Quincy Adams (1767–1848)
6th president of the United States of America;
his final words

"It is beautiful."

—Elizabeth Barrett Browning (1806–1861)
Poet and wife of Robert Browning; her final words

"You can kill us, but not hurt us."

—Justin Martyr (103–165)
Christian intellectual and martyr; in a letter to
the emperor of Rome, before his beheading

DYING WITHOUT CHRIST

"I would give worlds, if I had them, that *Age of Reason* had not been published. O Lord, help me! Christ, help me! . . . If ever the devil had an agent, I have been that one."

—**Thomas Paine** (1737–1809)
British pamphleteer, revolutionary, deist, intellectual, and author of Age of Reason; *spoken shortly before his death*

"You need not tell me there is no God for I know there is one, and that I am in His presence. You need not tell me there is no hell. I feel myself already slipping. . . . I know I am lost forever! Oh! That fire! Oh the insufferable pangs of hell."

—**Sir Francis Newport** (1620–1708)
First earl of Bradford, English nobleman, and politician; spoken shortly before his death

"What blood shed! What murders! What evil counsel I have followed! O my God, forgive me . . . I am lost! I am lost!"

—**King Charles IX of France** (1550–1574)
King of France at the time of the bloody killing of thousands of Protestant Hugenot Christians, that became known as the St. Bartholomew's Day massacre; spoken as he was dying

"I am abandoned by God and man! I will give you half of what I am worth if you will give me six months' life." [Voltaire said this to Dr. Trochin who told him it could not be done.] "Then I shall go to hell; and you will go with me."

—Francois Voltaire (1694–1778)
French philosopher and skeptic; as witnessed by his nurse,
"Voltaire died a terrible death, for all the money in Europe
I wouldn't want to see another unbeliever die.
All night long he cried for forgiveness."

"All this is now lost, finally, irrevocably lost. All is dark and doubtful."

—Edward Gibbon (1737–1794)
English historian, member of Parliament, agnostic,
and author of Decline and Fall of the Roman Empire;
his last words

"The science to which I pinned my faith is bankrupt. . . . And now they look at me and witness the great tragedy of an atheist who has lost his faith."

—George Bernard Shaw (1856–1950)
American playwright; written shortly before his death

"While I lived, I provided for everything but death; now I must die, and am unprepared to die."

—Cesare Borgia (1475–1507)
Italian Duke of Valentinois, the illegitimate son of
Pope Alexander VI; spoken just before his death

ANCIENT TRUTH

THE NICENE CREED

For three centuries fierce persecution was inflicted upon the early Christians by Roman authorities and emperors. Such leaders attempted to destroy this group of Christians, sometimes called "the way," as they persisted in following the teachings of a resurrected Christ. Many followers were imprisoned, brutally killed, or forced to fight wild animals in the Roman Coliseum.

Still the early church only continued to grow in faith and number. Undeniably because of Christ, the universe had changed in 33 AD.

In 313 AD Emperor Constantine issued the Edict of Milan, officially legalizing Christianity. Shortly thereafter, in 325 AD, a creed was formed to espouse faith in Christ and consolidate the basic beliefs of the early church.

Throughout all centuries, this beautifully crafted creed has been universally agreed upon by Christians of all traditions including Catholic, Protestant, Orthodox, and others. Appearing in the hymnals and worship rituals of virtually all Christian communions, the Nicene Creed speaks of our common beliefs and oneness in Christ. This text is the revised version of 381 AD.

The Nicene Creed

WE BELIEVE IN ONE GOD, THE FATHER, THE Almighty, of all that is, seen and unseen.

We believe in one Lord, Jesus Christ, the only Son of God, eternally begotten of the Father, God from God, Light from Light, true God from true God, begotten, not made, of one Being with the Father. Through him all things were made.

For us and for our salvation, he came down from heaven: by the power of the Holy Spirit he became incarnate from the Virgin Mary, and was made man. For our sake he was crucified under Pontius Pilate; he suffered death and was buried. On the third day he rose again in accordance with the Scriptures; he ascended into heaven, and is seated at the right hand of the Father. He will come again in glory to judge the living and the dead, and his kingdom will have no end.

We believe in the Holy Spirit, the Lord, the giver of life, who proceeds from the Father and the Son. With the Father and the Son he is worshipped and glorified. He has spoken through the prophets.

We believe in one holy catholic [universal] and apostolic Church. We acknowledge one baptism for the forgiveness of sins. We look for the resurrection of the dead, and the life of the world to come. Amen.

Promise of a Messiah

The Prophecy of Isaiah

In 1947, a young goat herder living near the Northwest shore of the Dead Sea in Israel, threw a rock into a cave and he heard something shatter. What broke was an ancient jar containing the greatest archeological discovery of the twentieth century, the Dead Sea Scrolls.

Among the scrolls were nineteen parchment and papyrus copies of the writings of the prophet Isaiah more than one thousand years older than any previously discovered. This finding, when compared to more modern manuscripts, proved the ancient Jewish scribes recorded history with astoundingly absolute accuracy.

Concerning a coming Jewish Messiah, the prophet Isaiah poetically, beautifully, and accurately describes the events of the Messiah's life on earth.

The following prophecies from Isaiah 53, recorded in 750 BC, are in **bold**. The astounding fulfillments of these prophecies by Jesus Christ nearly eight hundred years later, 30–33 AD, are in *italics*.

Isaiah 53

750 BC
Who has believed our message and to whom has the arm of the Lord been revealed?

> 30–33 AD
> "After Jesus had done all these miraculous signs in their presence, they still would not believe in Him" (John 12:37).

He grew up before Him like a tender shoot, and like a root out of dry ground. He had no beauty or majesty to attract us to Him, nothing in His appearance that we should desire Him.

> "Only in his hometown and in his own house is a prophet without honor" said Jesus (Matt. 13:57).

He was despised and rejected by men,

> "Again the Jews picked up stones to stone Him" (John 10:31).

a man of sorrows,

> "Jesus wept" (John 11:35).

and familiar with suffering.

> "Foxes have holes and birds of the air have nests, but the Son of Man has no place to lay His head" declared Jesus (Matt. 8:20).

Like one from whom men hide their faces He was despised, and we esteemed Him not.

> "You, a mere man, claim to be God" said the accusing crowd (John 10:33).

Surely He took up our infirmities

> "Filled with compassion, Jesus reached out His hand and touched the man [the leper], 'I am willing,' He said. 'Be clean!' Immediately the leprosy left him and he was cured" (Mark 1:41–42).

and carried our sorrows,

> "He had compassion on them and healed their sick" (Matt. 14:14).

yet we considered Him stricken by God, smitten by Him, and afflicted.

> *"Then they spit in His face and struck Him with their fists. Others slapped him"* (Matt. 26:67).

But He was pierced for our transgressions,

> *"One of the soldiers pierced Jesus' side with a spear"* (John 19:34).

He was crushed for our iniquities; the punishment that brought us peace was upon Him,

> *"Then Pilate took Jesus and had Him flogged"* (John 19:1).

and by His wounds we are healed.

> *"Jesus turned and saw her. 'Take heart, daughter,' He said, 'your faith has healed you.' And the woman was healed from that moment"* (Matt. 9:22).

We all, like sheep, have gone astray, each of us has turned to his own way;

> *"From this time many of His disciples turned back and no longer followed Him"* (John 6:66).

and the Lord has laid on Him the iniquity of us all.

> *"The Son of Man must be delivered into the hands of sinful men, be crucified and on the third day be raised again"* warned Jesus (Luke 24:7).

He was oppressed and afflicted, yet He did not open His mouth;

> *"He gave no answer"* (Matt. 27:12).

He was led like a lamb to the slaughter,

> *"They bound Him, led Him away . . ."* (Matt. 27:2).

And as a sheep before her shearers is silent, so He did not open His mouth.

> *"But Jesus remained silent"* (Matt. 26:63).

By oppression and judgment He was taken away.

> *"Then seizing Him, they led Him away and took Him into the house of the high priest"* (Luke 22:54).

And who can speak of His descendants?

> *"For whoever does the will of My Father in heaven is My brother and sister and mother"* said Jesus (Matt. 12:50).

For He was cut off from the land of the living;

> *"With a loud cry, Jesus breathed His last"* (Mark 15:37).

for the transgression of My people He was stricken.

> *"Then they spit in His face and struck Him with their fists. Others slapped Him and said, 'Prophesy to us, Christ. Who hit you?'"* (Matt. 26:67–68).

He was assigned a grave with the wicked, and with the rich in His death,

> *"A rich man from Arimathea, named Joseph . . . took the body, wrapped it in a clean linen cloth, and placed it in his own new tomb that he had cut out of the rock"* (Matt. 27:57–60).

though He had done no violence, nor was any deceit in His mouth.

> *"I have examined Him in your presence and have found no basis for your charges against Him,"* [said Pilate the Roman governor] (Luke 23:14).

Yet it was the Lord's will to crush Him and cause Him to suffer,

> *"They stripped Him and put a scarlet robe on Him, and then twisted together a crown of thorns and set it on His head. . . . They spit on Him, and took the staff and struck Him on the head again and again"* (Matt. 27:28–30).

and though the Lord makes His life a guilt offering, He will see His offspring

> *"Still, many in the crowd put their faith in Him"* (John 7:31).

and prolong His days, and the will of the Lord will prosper in His hand.

> *"Many followed Him, and He healed all their sick"* (Matt. 12:15).

After the suffering of His soul, He will see light of life

> *"I am leaving the world and going back to the Father"* declared Jesus (John 16:28).

and be satisfied; by His knowledge my righteous servant will justify many,

> "Whoever lives and believes in Me will never die" said Jesus (John 11:26).

and He will bear their iniquities.

> "Look, the Lamb of God, who takes away the sin of the world!" [said John the Baptist upon seeing Jesus] (John 1:29).

Therefore I will give Him a portion among the great,

> "All authority in heaven and on earth has been given to Me" said Jesus (Matt. 28:18).

and He will divide the spoils with the strong,

> "Whoever believes and is baptized will be saved, but whoever does not believe will be condemned" warned Jesus (Mark 16:16).

because He poured out His life unto death,

> "Jesus called out with a loud voice, 'Father, into Your hands I commit My spirit.' When He had said this, He breathed His last" (Luke 23:46).

and was numbered with the transgressors.

> "It is written: 'And he was numbered with the transgressors'; and I tell you that this must be fulfilled in me. Yes, what is written about me is reaching its fulfillment" said Jesus (Luke 22:37).

> "There they crucified Him, along with the criminals—one on His right, the other on His left" (Luke 23:33).

For He bore the sin of many, and made intercession for the transgressors.

> "Jesus said, 'Father, forgive them, for they do not know what they are doing'" (Luke 23:34).

Epilogue

The ancient story you have read is the most widely documented and attested to in all of human history. Within these pages you have also discovered overwhelming and unprecedented validation from scores of the world's greatest leaders, educators, and scientists across the generations. Throughout time, untold multitudes from all nations and races have adopted the creeds, merits, and truths contained herein.

The Truth Diary has sought to prove, with the purest evidence and the truest testimony, God's plan for this dying world and His never-ending love for you. Receiving and accepting this message can bring you peace, love, joy, and eternal security.

If this document has found its way into your hands, please allow it to reach into your innermost being. Ponder the message of who you are, why you are here, and what will become of you.

The warnings of peril contained within this book are not to be disregarded. Most certainly, and above all, the eternal treasures in this book are yours, simply for the asking.